CW01639405

As I Loved You

Building relationships with God and each other

Susan Hardwick

Kevin Mayhew

First published in 1998 by
KEVIN MAYHEW LTD
Rattlesden
Bury St Edmunds
Suffolk IP30 0SZ

0 1 2 3 4 5 6 7 8 9

ISBN 1 84003 234 0
Catalogue No 1500221

Cover design and illustrations by Karen Perrins
Typesetting by Louise Selfe
Printed and bound in Great Britain.

About the Author

Susan Hardwick is an Anglican priest in Coventry Diocese. She trained for the ordained ministry at Queen's College, Birmingham (1982-5), since when she has worked for the Coventry Diocese and the wider Church in various areas of ministry. Susan Hardwick was priested in 1994 at Coventry Cathedral.

She is married to an Anglican priest and has two grown-up children.

Susan Hardwick is the author of *A Weaving of Peace, Woven Fine, You Visited Me, Lifelines, Rest in Peace, Cross + Words, Why, God?, Dare to Hope*, and several books for children and young people, all published by Kevin Mayhew Ltd.

Acknowledgements

Bible quotations are taken from:

The Holy Bible, *New International Version*, © Copyright 1973, 1978, 1984 by International Bible Society, published by Hodder and Stoughton Ltd. All rights reserved. 'NIV' is a registered trademark of International Bible Society. UK trademark number 1448790. Used by permission.

The New Jerusalem Bible published and © Copyright 1985 by Darton, Longman and Todd Ltd. and Doubleday and Co Inc. and used by permission of the publisher.

The Message © by Eugene H. Peterson, 1993, 1994, 1995, 1996, 1997. Used by permission of NavPress Publishing Group.

The extract from *The Song of the Bird* by Anthony de Mello SJ is quoted by permission of Gujarat Sahitya Prakash, Anand, Gujarat, 388001, India.

About ths Book

This book on relationships is divided into four main parts:

Part one reflects on Jesus' earthly relationships, both personal and with a whole range of people whom he met as he went about teaching and preaching, healing and raising – and what each of these encounters teaches us about our own relationships.

Part two reflects on the tremendous truth that each one of us as a unique human being, each living creature, and all of God's creation, is created by God's love, to love.

We are, as human beings, interwoven and interdependent one with another.

Part three consists of prayers for use by people in various situations and relationships.

Relationships are not just an earthly experience. Part four begins by reflecting on the Trinity of Love: the relationship between God the Father, his Son Jesus Christ, and the Holy Spirit – and how each of us is invited to become a partner in this eternal dance of love which sustains creation in being. It ends by looking at God's relationship with all he has made.

Contents

The First Word 9

I Am One. I Am Many 11

Relationships . . . 15

PART ONE

Jesus' Relationships 19

with his family 20

with his Nazareth neighbours 22

with his friends: 26

– his women friends 28

– his men friends 31

The consequences of being in relationship with him 33

The relationship of Jesus with God the Father 36

Checklist

Some of the qualities Jesus displayed in his relationships 37

PART TWO

We Are . . . 43

PART THREE

Prayers 55

Carer 55

Friend 57

Neighbour 59

Offspring:
- Child/Teenager 61
- Adult 63

Parent 65
Partner 68
Worker 70
Endings 72
Beginnings 74
Separation 75
Hurts 76
Joys 77
God and us 79

PART FOUR
Three-Way Love: 85
One-in-three: I AM . . . God 85
Three-in-one: WE ARE . . . the Father, the Son, and the Holy Spirit 87
Four-Way Love: 90
WE ARE . . . the Trinity – and us 90
God's relationship with all he has made 91

The Last Word 95

The First Word

We are born, we live and we die in relationship. This is true for even the most solitary of us.

Human relationships are not clear-cut. You don't know when or where they are going to begin, or when or where they will end. You don't know where they might lead you; how they will change on the way, or how they will affect and change you – indeed, this uncertainty is one of the great anticipations of any new relationship.

Throughout our lives, our inner as well as our outer relationships are many. Much of the task of life is to try both to bring order, harmony and wholeness to our often fragmented and disordered inner selves, and to be an agent, a bearer of peace and justice, harmony and wholeness to those amongst whom God has set us.

The world and its experience is reflected within each one of us. Fragmented relationships and communities are mirrored by our own inner experience: each one of us is a whole world in miniature.

As well as celebrating the good things within ourselves, we need also to embrace the various areas of darkness with the light of understanding; not denying their existence, but acknowledging their presence in order to bring healing and wholeness.

If you wish to change the world, change first yourself, said Jesus (Matthew 7:3-5).

Throughout the book, links are made with our own experience, and what lessons we can learn about how to be more creative within these relationships.

Susan Hardwick

I Am One. I Am Many

We are all in a multitude of relationships. Some are fixed and permanent. Others relate to particular periods of one's life. The following exercise helps to illustrate this.

Picture one – represents the various external relationships in your life, for example: child or offspring/parent/friend/employee/work colleague/neighbour/carer and so on.

In each shape, write one category which is relevant to your life now. Of course, some of the categories may embrace a number of individual relationships.

Picture two – As well as our external relationships, each of us has a variety of relationships within ourselves; internal moods, attitudes, inclinations, and so on. Some are negative and life-denying, for example, greed or hate, and cause us anxiety, pain, stress, fear. Others are positive, creative and life-giving, for example, generosity and love. And yet others can be either one or the other depending upon the situation and content, for example, hope and dreams.

We are each a community of selves, which are often at war with each other but which, within the love of Christ, have the potential to become more and more integrated – until Christ is able to proclaim, as he did to so many in his earthly life: 'Your faith has made you whole!'

In each of the pictures, you may need to draw more shapes. If the exercise is done prayerfully, it can be very illuminating. It is also a good idea to return to the exercise on several occasions, and to add in any further examples of which you have thought.

Picture One

Picture Two

RELATIONSHIPS . . .

. . . are a lifelong task which can be heavenly – infinitely enriching and rewarding as well as, at times, infinitely demanding and costly . . . and sometimes, of course, they can feel like hell!

Relationships never stay static. They are constantly changing and evolving. They can ask that we dig into our deepest selves for the resources needed to nurture them. They ask for our vulnerability, our time, our commitment, our patience and long-suffering, our forgiveness, our generosity and much, much more.

More than anything, they ask for our love. Not only the spontaneous love which is called forth by a strong sense of mutual attraction and empathy, but more particularly and especially the disciplined love which can carry on loving even when there is not obviously much to love. The sort of love which is, above all, about constancy and commitment and faithfulness.

When we love like that, we are treading on holy ground, for Christ has been there before us. Love like this is familiar territory to him, for it is the way in which he loved those with whom he came into contact in his earthly life, the way in which he loved the world enough to die for us all, and the way in which he loves each one of us now through his Spirit.

When we respond to this Jesus love, when we open our hearts to receive it, our whole world changes. Like a film moving from black and white to full colour, everything is transformed and given myriad new tones and shades of meaning and depth.

So, if we seek to change, deepen and enrich our relationships with each other and with God, we can do no better than first to reflect on how the earthly Jesus related to his heavenly Father, and to those around him.

If we take the lessons learned, we can apply them to our own relationships. We can see each of them and the people involved through Jesus' eyes, so to speak. If we ask Jesus to become a partner in each of our relationships, we create our own eternal triangle of love, centred on God. We create our own holy trinity – just as Jesus the Son, God the Father and the Holy Spirit are the Holy Trinity of Love.

Later on, we will look at the beautiful and awesome relationship of this Trinity of Love, and how it sustains our very being in existence.

Now, though, we turn to our inspirer and guide and example, and see how Jesus lived out his various relationships whilst he was here on earth, in order that we may learn from him. If we compare and contrast his ways with ours, we may understand a little more about how best we may live out our own relationships.

PART ONE

Jesus' Relationships

Jesus, in his earthly life, seems to have sought out those who were considered very ordinary, of no special account in the eyes of others nor, most probably, in their own eyes. He elevated each one to the extra-ordinary by his deep appreciation and valuing and loving.

He saw through to the centre of people with new eyes and turned them inside out. Figs grew upon thorns; perceptions were changed; self-respect bloomed where formerly there was none; cowards became brave; lepers were embraced and became healthy and whole.

He laughed and rejoiced with those who were happy, and shared the sadness of those who sorrowed. He gave each person whose life he touched a new identity, and a new sense of worth.

All sorts of people were probably also drawn to him for all kinds of personal reasons as, in him, they found the perfect complement to all their own shortcomings of personality and needs. He was like the missing jigsaw pieces needed to make the picture complete.

The Incarnation means that Jesus was a real human being of flesh and blood, feelings and emotions and needs, hopes and dreams. He wasn't playacting; only pretending to be human. He was not like the Greek gods who sometimes, as the old myths and fables had it, became a human being but retained all their divine privileges and power. The humanity of Jesus was absolutely real.

The Greek word used for 'being' and 'form' – as in human being and human form – describes the very essence of humanity. So, when we, like St Paul, describe Jesus as being in the form of God, we mean that he is essentially and absolutely God – and yet he took upon himself, and into himself, the nature of the very least of human beings in those days: a slave.

Jesus was, in fact, the most real human being who has ever lived. He holds up to us an example of what it means to be truly human, and what it means to have divinely human relationships. That being so, he knew all about the difficulties and joys of relationships.

So, when we look to Jesus for example and inspiration, it is in the knowledge that he knows all about how it is and how it feels, for he has been there before us.

> Jesus – tempted in every way just as we are, yet was without sin.
> *Hebrews 4:15b (NIV)*

Like a pebble dropped into a pool, the ripples caused by him widened and widened until they have left no part of the world unaffected by his impact.

We'll begin at the beginning: Jesus, as a boy, with his family.

Jesus with his family

When Mary and Joseph took the baby Jesus to the Temple in Jerusalem, forty days after his birth, they were met by Simeon,

> a good man who lived in the prayerful expectancy of help for Israel. And the Holy Spirit was on him. The Holy Spirit had shown him that he would see the Messiah of God before he died . . . Simeon took [the child Jesus] into his arms and blessed God: '. . .With my own eyes I've seen your salvation . . .', he said.
> *Luke 2:25f (The Message)*

He told Mary that a sword would pierce her heart on account of her son. Many years later, his words must have echoed particularly painfully as, quite often bewildered, she watched her son's living out of his vocation.

There was much she did not understand at the time it happened. But her mother-love never faltered. She may not always have understood immediately, but her love of him and belief in him were total and unswerving.

Jesus, for his part, must have had an innate, if at first subconscious, awareness of his own destiny, which grew into maturity as he grew physically, mentally, emotionally and spiritually. Luke's Gospel tells us he was an obedient son, highly thought of by everyone . . .

> . . . he lived obediently with them . . . And Jesus matured, growing up in both body and spirit, blessed by both God and people.
> *Luke 2:51-52 (The Message)*

From all we read of Jesus, it is obvious that he had an easy way with people, instantly knew how to relate at a very deep level, and liked socialising, parties and celebrations. He clearly also had a very strong and focused personality.

So – was it hard having such an extra-ordinary person at the very centre of the family?

And, if his parents did not always understand him, and what he said and did – as we read in Luke 2:41f, about the twelve-year old Jesus in the Temple in Jerusalem – was he even more of an enigma to his younger brothers and sisters?

I imagine they must have looked up to him and admired their big brother for all that he was but, at the same time, did they feel they were growing up in his shadow? Did they feel he was an impossible act to follow?

I imagine Jesus would have been deeply aware of all these things, and would have been very sensitive to the needs of his siblings. I imagine him encouraging the shy ones, gently teasing the bumptious ones, building up the ones with low self-esteem; being generous, and standing aside, in order to give the others the room they, too, needed in order to expand as people and to grow and to blossom into their full potential.

I imagine that his home and his family was the natural seedbed in which he learned about giving and receiving love:

in the give and take of family life – and the place where he developed and refined his innate sensitivity to the needs of others.

We don't know when Joseph died. But I wonder whether it was one of the reasons why Jesus did not leave home until he was 30 years of age; an unusually late time for a Jewish man. Was he taking care of his mother, sisters and brothers, until others were ready to take over the task, and would not leave until then – not even to save the world?

And his son-love for his mother never dimmed. His last thought, as he died on the Cross, was for his mother's well-being, and who should protect her and care for her from now on. For, in the Jewish world of that time, widows had no status or identity other than that conferred upon them by their male relatives.

Jesus with his Nazareth neighbours

It is easy to believe that Jesus was a natural leader, even in his earliest days.

I imagine him as a boy, full of high spirits, enjoying everything he did – other children attracted to him because of the joy he radiated – and revelling in God's creation. Very happy to be with his friends, but just as happy to be on his own. Every day full of beauty and of miracles, because the world is beautiful and miraculous.

When, in his public ministry, he placed a child in the midst of his disciples and spoke about childhood innocence, I wonder if he was also thinking back to his own childhood, and the years of happy abandonment before he became fully aware of the tremendous task which lay upon him and before him.

> The people brought children to Jesus, hoping he might touch them. The disciples shooed them off. But Jesus was irate and let them know it. 'Don't push these children away. Don't ever get between them and me. These children are at the very centre of life in the kingdom. Mark this: unless you accept God's kingdom in the simplicity of a child, you'll never get in.' Then, gathering the children up in his arms, he laid his hands of blessing on them.
> *Mark 10:13f. (The Message)*

Then, as he got older, his Nazareth neighbours must have wondered why such a personable young man was not betrothed as was the custom, sometimes from an early age – the curiosity and speculation gathering momentum as the years went by. There must have been many a parent who would have been delighted to see their daughter wedded to him, for he would have been quite a catch.

I imagine him quietly and cleverly and good-humouredly fielding any curious enquiries; just as so often he did later in his public ministry, when challenged by the barbed remarks or the slyly concocted, seemingly innocent questions which were, in reality, designed to catch him out.

But, because he was at peace with himself, he would have felt at peace with his neighbours – even when he did not agree with them or had to oppose them, sometimes very strongly, over a particular issue.

However, even he came to know the deep hurt of not being appreciated or valued by them for what he had become, or for what he did, in his public ministry.

At first, they had been impressed with his gifts of healing and his wisdom. But then, when he stepped beyond the boundaries of their approval and presumed to challenge them, their admiration turned to homicidal rage. They could not cope with Jesus' honesty and integrity.

So long as he had a little boy's respect for them, they were prepared to indulge him, but there *were* limits . . .

> . . . They sprang to their feet and hustled him out of the town; and they took him up to the brow of the hill their town was built on, intending to throw him off the cliff, but he passed straight through the crowd and walked away.
> *Luke 4:29, 30 (NJB)*

How desperately hurt he must have been.

These were the people amongst whom he had grown up; his extended family. In the Jewish communities of those days, there was a great sense of mutual concern: the wellbeing of your neighbour was your responsibility, and your wellbeing was theirs.

I have stood on the brow of that hill, and looked down at Nazareth, in the valley far below. It is, indeed, a fearsome drop.

Today, the narrow streets that wind their way up to the top of the hill are lined with simple dwellings and, as you pass, people watch you with a detached curiosity. Children dance along in front and behind you, calling and trying to attract your attention. Did it look like this, I wondered, when Jesus passed by, dragged along by the angry, shouting mob?

Three years after this event, Jesus was to weep over Jerusalem for not accepting him and his teaching.

It was Palm Sunday; both the saddest and the happiest of days for him. Palms before his feet, the pain of knowledge like a deep wound in his heart that some of these same people now joyfully proclaiming 'Hosannah!' would very soon be shouting, 'Crucify him!'

Surely then, the rejection by his neighbours must have wrenched similar tears from deep within. Just before they dragged him from the Nazareth temple, in order to try to kill him on that sad day, he had said: 'Well, let me tell you something: no prophet is ever welcomed in his hometown'. *Luke 4:24 (The Message)*

However, as he hung on his Cross three years later on another hill, outside Jerusalem, he prayed that God the Father would forgive those who had put him there.

I imagine him on that hill outside Nazareth, walking away from all that had framed his life until then, tears of hurt and rejection streaming down his face, similarly praying:

> 'Father, forgive them. They don't know what they're doing'.
> *Luke 23:34a (The Message)*

Jesus seemed to receive and absorb all the pain and hurts inflicted upon him and allowed them to pass through him, being changed and rendered harmless as they went. He said . . .

> '. . . whatever enters the mouth goes into the stomach and then out of the body. But the things that come out of the mouth come from the heart and these make a person "unclean".'
> *Matthew 15:17, 18 (NIV adapted)*

As someone who sometimes stores up hurts and injustices, and then finds release for them much later, maybe at inappropriate and irrelevant moments which have little or no connection to the incident, I find this *very* challenging indeed.

The immensity of heart, the generosity of spirit and the depth of love required so to speak is awe-inspiring.

Even so, if he felt that some injustice or lie – particularly if directed towards others – needed challenging, he would speak out clearly and confidently.

Turning the other cheek did not seem to mean always silent acceptance, rather a calm, prayerful assessment of how best to meet face to face with a particular situation, confront any wrong within it, with the kind of response that would prove most likely to defeat the evil. Sometimes that might mean a dignified silence which refused to stoop to the level of the wrong, and sometimes that would mean speaking out, or taking appropriate action.

Jesus with his friends

> 'No one can have greater love than to lay down his life for his friends. You are my friends, if you do what I command you . . .'
> *John 15:13, 14 (NJB)*

. . . So said Jesus, at the Last Supper, just a few hours before he went out to die for us all.

His death split open infinity, and his love spilled out to embrace the world for evermore.

Because of this, his words were not only addressed to his disciples gathered there in the Upper Room on that fateful night, but to *all* who follow him and who obey his commandments.

And so, when we answer his call we, too, enter into that blessed group of people to whom Jesus's words are spoken: 'You are my friends'.

I think it cannot have been an easy thing to be a friend of Jesus. It must have been both wonderful and devastating at the same time.

Just imagine what it would have been like to be continually challenged by all that he was as a person. To be faced by absolute goodness, and to know that there is absolutely no way in which you could match up, would be like having a mirror constantly before you reflecting all the flaws of which, until then, you'd either been blissfully unaware, or else had managed successfully to deny.

To acknowledge someone as being a friend puts them on an equal footing. To keep a friendship balanced, there needs to be give and take by both sides. There are all sorts of implicit assumptions built in to a friendship: shared values and ideals maybe; shared interests or expectations.

To call someone your friend is to pay that person a great compliment – at least, so far as you are concerned! It is to say that there are many things about that person which you feel distinguish them, which single them out, as special.

Jesus seems to have needed, and to have had, a variety of friendships, which he valued and which sustained and nurtured him in a variety of ways. Each fulfilled a particular need, for Jesus – unlike many strong and self-sufficient people – knew the grace of being able to receive, as well as the joy of giving.

What a privilege it must have been to hear Jesus saying, 'I need you'. Perhaps not in just those words but because, in his sensitivity to the need of others to be needed, he opened himself up and made himself vulnerable.

When the young woman, some say it was Mary Magdalene, broke a jar of expensive perfume – which must have cost her a great deal in more than one way – in order to anoint Jesus' head and feet, there was much criticism from those around.

But Jesus received the act of love with pleasure and understanding, and he defended her actions . . .

> . . . While Jesus was in Bethany in the home of a man known as Simon the Leper, a woman came to him with an alabaster jar of very expensive perfume, which she poured on his head as he was reclining at the table. When the disciples saw this, they were indignant. 'Why this waste?' they asked. 'This perfume could have been sold at a high price and the money given to the poor'. Aware of this, Jesus said to them, 'Why are you bothering this woman? She has done a beautiful thing to me . . . I tell you the truth, wherever this gospel is preached throughout the world, what she has done will also be told, in memory of her'.
> *Matthew 26:6-10, 13 (NIV)*

Jesus' host, Simon, must, in fact, have been cured of his leprosy – probably by Jesus – otherwise he wouldn't have been mixing in society: he would still have been an ill, isolated and feared man.

I wonder, did Simon see Jesus as a private possession of his, and Jesus' visit to his home an ego-tripping opportunity to show him off? Was he jealous that his hospitality had been upstaged by this woman?

But Simon was to learn, just as we all must, that Jesus befriends us not only for our own sakes but also in order that we, in our turn, may make him known to others.

And Jesus' disciples: even they, too, had got it wrong.

However, Jesus manages to hold together all these disparate elements – Simon the ex-leper, the disciples and the woman; manages to do some important teaching without alienating anyone, whilst never once appearing to withdraw the love and acceptance with which he surrounded each one. Quite a feat!

And yet, Jesus does this sort of thing time and time and time again, without once compromising his high expectations or his integrity.

Jesus always seemed to practise what he preached. He made it seem so deceptively easy.

Feeling just as we do, though, he must have known all the same hurts, the same disappointments, the same bewilderment we all feel when our friends let us down, or don't come up to our expectations and hopes of them. The deeper the love, the greater is the pain.

However, the same love and bountiful generosity of heart which could pray for forgiveness for those who so cruelly hurt him at the very moment he was being nailed to the Cross, I imagine would have flowed in, supporting him in his sadness and washing his wounds clean, ready for healing.

Jesus' model of friendship was obviously about being totally true to the relationship: about being steadfast and wholly reliable; about respecting and caring for the other enough to say it always the way it really was – not in a confrontational way, but never being sycophantic either.

It was about being real. *He* was about being real.

Jesus with his women friends

Jesus, in his obvious valuing of women, reached far beyond the bounds of convention of that time. He seemed to have found the perfect complement to his personality and his masculinity in his friendship with the women in his life.

There were those to whom he went when he was weary of the open road, the travel, the pressing crowds, the endless need. Mary and Martha's home obviously was just such a resting place for Jesus, and I imagine him arriving there with a great sense of pleasure and relief; relaxing, unwinding, allowing the pent-up tiredness to be released.

I picture him reclining, enjoying the lovingly prepared food, revelling in the tender care and solace and love with which the sisters surrounded him, and appreciating the fragrant and feminine environment. Warming himself both in the glow of the fire and their friendship. After experiencing rejection, opposition and scorn on his travels, knowing the wonderful affirmation of being listened to with rapt attention, each word valued because it was he who spoke it.

He would know he was always welcome, and be aware any request for hospitality would be met with delight. Then, strengthened and refreshed, he would go on the road again, knowing that this retreat with his friends Martha and Mary was there, waiting for the next time he needed it, and them.

He could be sure, too, their tender love travelled with him and that they would hold him constantly in their prayers and in their hearts.

The Bible speaks of various women, coming like his male disciples from all walks of life and sections of society, who followed Jesus, tending his needs and, those who were able, providing from their own purses. Some are named:

> Joanna the wife of Chuza, the manager of Herod's household; Susanna; and many others. These women were helping to support [Jesus and the disciples] out of their own means.
> *Luke 8:3 (NIV)*

> Some women were watching [the crucifixion] from a distance. Among them were Mary Magdalene, Mary

> the Mother of James the younger and of Joses, and Salome. In Galilee, these women had followed him, and cared for his needs. Many other women who had come up with him to Jerusalem were also there.
> *Mark 15:40, 41 (NIV)*

And – although not a 'friend' in the same way as the others, of course – the Syro-Phoenician women. She was a very special person, in that she won an argument with Jesus and played a key role in his thinking out of his mission. She also illustrates Jesus' willingness to learn from those whom he came to teach. (See Mark 7:24f.)

From all we read, it seems clear that Mary Magdalene occupied a particularly special place in his heart. His compassion aroused first by her harsh treatment at the hands of her accusers, I imagine he was subsequently drawn to her fiery temperament and her strong and definite personality.

At a time when a woman had no status beyond that bestowed upon her by the men in her life, Mary's assertion of her independence, and her defiance of the unjust male status quo, must have appealed to him.

In Mary, Jesus perhaps recognised a fire and a passion similar to his own which, if it could be redirected, would be a force for much good. He would have seen her great potential and he would have loved her, both for what she could become as well as for her unredeemed self – which, indeed, is the way he loves each one of us.

I imagine Jesus fully appreciating her physical beauty, in just the same way he would fully appreciate and marvel at *any* beauty – whether it was a flower, a sunset, or a person – because any beauty is a gift from God and, therefore, to be valued and wondered at for itself.

For Mary, it must have been a devastating but wonderful experience to be loved by such a man, not for her body but for her inner self, and for her potential.

At first, I guess she would have been cynical and suspicious, wondering just how long it would be before he, too, like most of the other men she had known, made physical demands upon her. But, as time passed and the love between them deepened, as is the way of all true friendships, she would have come to know that *this* relationship was different. *This* relationship was like no other she had ever known.

As her trust in Jesus grew and her defences fell away, it must have felt like a fresh spring breeze, perfume-laden with the fragrance and promise of new young flowers, blowing through her world-weary and battered and stale emotional life – refreshing, cleansing, restoring, renewing and recreating – as she felt herself set free from all that had trapped her and held her in thrall until then, and as she began to blossom into the person she was always meant to be.

And that is how God asks us to love each one of those whom he gives us: to love them in such a way that sets them free, with the generosity of a Jesus.

Jesus with his men friends

I wonder if, in fact, it was harder for men to be friends with Jesus, than for women. Women would not be challenged by some of the comparisons that men, being of the same sex, could draw between themselves and Jesus. And yet, Jesus obviously had a variety of close male friends. Primarily, presumably, these would have been the twelve disciples with whom he travelled and with whom he shared his life and public ministry for three years.

Peter, James and John seemed especially close to him. He chose them and took them apart from the others to witness the raising of Jairus' daughter (Luke 8:40f.), and the Transfiguration (Luke 9:28f), and he asked them to keep watch whilst he prayed in anguish in the Garden of Gethsemane (Mark 14:32f).

Perhaps he was preparing them for the particularly high-profile ministries which they would exercise after his death: James as leader of the Church in Jerusalem, John in Ephesus, and Peter in Rome.

John, as we read in the Gospel of John, felt he held a special place in Jesus' heart; maybe because he was the youngest, and/or perhaps they had a mental or spiritual rapport.

It was to John that Jesus entrusted the care of his mother, as he was dying on the Cross. And when Peter and John run to Jesus' tomb and find it empty, John appears to realise immediately its implications and so, probably throughout Jesus' ministry, similarly understood quicker, more deeply, more intuitively than the others the things about which Jesus strove to teach his disciples.

And what of those other disciples? You get the sense, from what is said in the Bible, that Jesus had an individual and unique relationship with each one of them; a relationship which reflected the marrying together of Jesus' personality with that of the particular disciple in question: Matthew the tax collector, Simon the Zealot, the spontaneous Nathaniel, the loyal and honest Thomas, who had the courage also to give voice to his doubts . . . each feeling valued for who and what they were, but, also, challenged to become what they were yet not.

And other men, outside that group?

What of Lazarus, over whose death Jesus wept? (John 11:1f)

And Simon the Leper: was he, too, privileged to call himself a friend of Jesus? If so, it is obvious that this status didn't protect him, as we have seen already – or *any* person, indeed, for that matter – from receiving Jesus' honest opinion. (Mark 14:3f)

And yet others, unnamed so far as we're concerned, but whom Jesus must have known well, and cared about.

It is this very openness and refusal to dissemble or pretend, which is one of the blocks upon which we build a relationship with Jesus which is as strong as rock.

As he knows already all the secrets of our hearts, all pretence is stripped away. What a relief! What a joy to know that we are loved despite all our failings. That he accepts and loves us as we are – yet, at the same time, profoundly believes in us, that we can become so much more.

The consequences of being in a relationship with Jesus

Yet it is Peter, not John, whom Jesus honours with the title of the Rock upon which his Church is to be built. Peter, who was the first of the twelve apostles to declare to Jesus . . .

> '. . . You have the message of eternal life, and we believe; we have come to know that you are the Holy One of God.'
> *John 6:68, 69 (NJB)*

Jesus always seems to have been able to balance emotion and objectivity. John may have been one of the people to whom emotionally and spiritually he was particularly attached, yet he did not let these feelings cloud his judgement.

In the impetuous, passionate-speaking Peter, Jesus early saw the potential, the latent qualities needed which he, Jesus, could then nurture and develop as they journeyed together – so that, at the right moment, the well-watered seed would blossom and bear much fruit.

Just, indeed, as Jesus hopes, plans, dreams to do with each of us. However, like Peter, we have to be prepared to change, to grow, to die to our old self in order that the new may come forth:

> '. . . unless a wheat grain falls into the earth and dies, it remains only a single grain, but if it dies it yields a rich harvest.'
> *John 12:24 (NJB)*

Or, put another way . . .

> '. . . Listen carefully. Unless a grain of wheat is buried in the ground, dead to the world, it is never any more than a grain of wheat. But if it is buried, it sprouts

> and reproduces itself many times over.
> In the same way, anyone who holds on to life just as it is destroys that life. But if you let it go, reckless in your love, you'll have it forever, real and eternal.'
> *John 12:24f (The Message)*

There is a whole world of mystery in the pain and the reality of letting go. So often it is so hard to do and yet, for those who dare to, very often a whole new world is revealed.

The old adage about one door closing before another can open really is true. As we grow older, our life experiences teach us this is so and yet, each time we are called upon to do it, the letting go can still be dreadfully difficult. It is as if we hold the superstitious belief that, as long as we are suspicious and cynical that nothing will be as good as that which we're giving up, all will be all right in the end. As soon as we start believing, though, in new doors opening they won't – or so we fear.

Although shaped and changed by his encounter, his friendship, his travelling with Jesus, Peter's nature doesn't seem to have been squashed at all. He is the same warm-hearted, hot-headed, irrepressible person at the Last Supper, with his spontaneous outbursts, as the man we initially met at the beginning of the Gospels: the first disciple whom Jesus calls to follow him.

His great and deep and constant love for Jesus is without doubt, as he reiterates on the shores of Lake Galilee, after the risen Christ meets with some of his disciples.

> Three times Jesus said to Simon Peter,
> 'Simon, son of John, do you love me more than these others do?'
> Three times Peter answered,
> 'Yes, Lord. You know I love you.'
> *John 21:15a (NJB)*

And when Peter realised that he had betrayed that love by denying he knew Jesus, because of fear of the consequences, he was inconsolable, and prostrate with grief (Matthew 26:69f; Luke 22:54f).

He touched rock bottom. He was shattered at this revelation of himself, and full of guilty despair.

But then he is restored by Jesus – who gives him the opportunity to declare his love again: one affirmation of love for each of the three denials that he had known Jesus.

Peter has faced the reality of himself. He is determined that, from now on, he will go on, in the power of Christ, to become the person Jesus had always intended him to be.

'. . . unless a wheat grain falls to the ground and dies . . .'

Jesus' friendship, Jesus' love, is never coercive. He allows Peter to develop at his own pace and to find his own way; Jesus, who constantly and gently challenges and points the way, but never forces.

In the end, it is up to Peter himself freely to decide whether he goes on, answers his calling, meets with his destiny and becomes Peter the Rock, the Fisher of People – or whether he goes back to being Simon, the fisher of fish.

Peter's story tells all of us, when we feel we have let Jesus down and have denied his love in us, that he is longing to pick us up, and to let us know that he loves us still.

Even when all the men – who, so short a time before, had been proud to walk by the side of Jesus and to share in the praise as he rode into Jerusalem on Palm Sunday – ran away and left Jesus at the hour of his great need, in the Garden of Gethsemane, he did not turn away from them, reject or harden his heart against them.

The sorrowing women, who had *not* run away, but who had stayed and faced the forces of darkness full on in their faithful vigil at the foot of the Cross, were eventually joined by John. He, presumably, had felt ashamed of his cowardice and had remustered his courage.

Jesus' faith in his friend obviously had not dimmed for he entrusts the care of the most beloved woman in his life, his mother, to John.

At the Last Supper, Jesus had predicted that Peter would deny knowing him. In reply, Peter had protested vigorously and earnestly, declaiming: 'If I have to die with you, I will never disown you.' *Mark 14:31 (NJB)*

And all the other disciples had said the same. Only hours later, though, they all melted away into the night, leaving Jesus on his own as he was arrested and taken away for questioning.

Yet Jesus, knowing Peter and the others well enough to predict this would happen, nevertheless had faith enough in them to believe that they would, indeed, recover and go on to bear *much* fruit. Fruit that would, in its turn, produce more fruit, which would then result in even more, and so on, until the coming of the Kingdom of Heaven on earth.

And what Jesus was to, and did for, his family, his neighbours, his women and men friends and those others he knew in his earthly life, he is, and does, for us today through his Spirit.

His constant friendship, his undying love, his honest encounter with each one of us at the very heart, the very centre, of our being is there for us to respond to – *if* that is what *we* choose – for God never coerces or forces. He has given us freedom to choose for ourselves, as to whether we accept him, or whether we reject him.

Jesus can be our passive partner, as it were. We can ignore the gentle call and invitation to follow him, so that he is neither impacting on, nor affecting us and what we do.

Or he can be our active, vibrant, vividly alive partner, giving each day, each moment of our lives strength, purpose, focus, energy, meaning. The choice is ours, each one of us, as to whether or not we open the door of our heart and invite him in – or whether we look away and content ourselves with the lesser gods of materialism, earthly success and so on.

Jesus' relationship with God the Father

However busy he was, however pressed by the crowds who came to him for teaching and for healing, Jesus never forgot his absolute need for, and dependence upon, his Heavenly Father.

He knew, through to the core of his being, that his Father sustained him in being, was his strength, his sustenance, the very wellspring from which he drew all his nourishment and nurture, his wisdom and his power.

Prayer preceded and surrounded all that he did, and especially his major decisions and actions. The Gospels record how he would often withdraw to a lonely place, where he could be on his own. Sometimes, his most trusted friends were invited along, too. Glory was always given to God.

If you read Luke's Gospel through in one sitting, it becomes very apparent just how important prayer is to Jesus, and how frequently he finds opportunities to pray; going off on his own, or with some of his disciples; in preparation for, or in the midst of, some task; giving thanks and praise; teaching prayer to others.

His public ministry begins with an extended period of prayer in the desert. His anguish at the prospect of the torment ahead of him he brings to the Father in prayer, in the Garden of Gethsemane. And his last words on the Cross are addressed to his Heavenly Father.

Checklist

Some of the qualities Jesus displayed in his relationships

- He valued people for themselves and their inner qualities.
- He was totally unimpressed with worldly status.
- Because he saw through to the inner potential of a person, and valued that, he brought it to life.
- He gave people self-respect, courage, self-worth, and a sense of their uniqueness.

- He made people feel whole: he completed their shortcomings, and drew together the opposites in others, giving them a sense of inner harmony.
- He was sensitive to the needs of others.
- He radiated inner peace, joy and wholeness.
- He met people where they were and shared their sorrows and their joys as if they were his own.
- He knew when to speak and when to be silent.
- He did not seek the limelight.
- He knew how to receive, as well as give, love.
- He knew the importance of needing others, of letting others minister to him, in order to keep the relationship in balance, and so that he did not have a power relationship which dominated others.
- He kept his vulnerability.
- He set people free.
- He gave people the space and freedom to be themselves, and to make their own choices.
- Similarly, he did not feel the need always to explain himself.
- Because he was at peace with himself he was at peace with others, even when he disagreed with what they said or their actions.
- He was totally honest. He respected and valued others enough not to dissemble. However, he would never be brutally honest: it was a creative, building-up honesty.
- He was ready to challenge evil again and again, whenever he saw it in its many forms.
- He did not 'use' his friends: casting them off or to one side when it was no longer expedient or helpful to have them as friends.

- He was very generous and self-giving with his time, his energy, his love.
- He was entirely consistent: expecting no more of others than he did of himself.
- He was steadfast, wholly reliable and trustworthy.
- He was friends with those whom he chose, not with those whom society or the current convention of the time would have expected.
- He was able to balance emotion with objectivity.
- He had great faith in people that they would find the strength to overcome their failures, and go on to bear much fruit: the belief often enabling the reality to be born.
- He freely forgave again, and again, and again: the same people, as well as forgiving others particular incidents or cruelties.
- He loved with a love which was never coercive.
- He loved with a love which set people free to be their best selves; the person they were always meant to be.
- All his relationships were framed and shot through with the consequence of his life of prayer, and his relationship with his Heavenly Father.

Can you think of more?

How do we compare?

Which of these qualities are reflected in our own relationships?

Part Two

We Are . . .

As human beings, interwoven and interdependent, one with another.

Not only does Jesus, through his Spirit, invite each one of us into a personal, living, loving relationship with him but, if asked, will enter into each of our relationships with one another.

Each human being, each living creature, all of God's creation from mighty mountains to the last blade of grass, was created by his love. His plan and purpose for us human beings is to love him, to love ourselves, to love each other.

From fingerprints to DNA patterns, again and again, our uniqueness and individuality is underlined. This uniqueness must have a very special purpose. Could it be that, like some vast jigsaw puzzle, if even the tiniest, seemingly most insignificant piece is missing, the picture is incomplete?

If that is so, then the size or importance or prominence of the jigsaw piece is not of such significance as received worldly 'wisdom' would like us to believe. A gap is a gap is a gap. Indeed, as St Paul said:

> 'It is precisely the parts of the body' (the jigsaw) 'that seem to be the weakest which are the indispensable ones.'
> *I Cor 12:22 (NJB)*

Although each of us is unique and individual, at the same time, our wellbeing and destiny are tightly interwoven with each other.

As with most analogies, our example of a jigsaw puzzle only takes us so far in our understanding. The pieces of a jigsaw are of a fixed, predetermined shape. Human beings, on the other hand, grow and change – and cause the wider society to do likewise. How important, then, that the growth and change is positive.

Like a mighty family of many different elements, the wellbeing of all depends on each, and the wellbeing of each depends on all. Maybe that sounds a bit like a party manifesto. However, it is what the Bible tells us again and again. It is also sound common sense, as the Bible so often proves itself to be.

We do not live in isolation – though some of us might be tempted to do so by burying our heads in the sands of indifference, trying to persuade ourselves that the problems and concerns of others are not really our business or concern.

We are intimately interconnected. Whatever I do, whatever I say, has an effect for good or bad, and its repercussions may be felt around the world. Metaphorically, I stamp my foot in petulant anger in England, and the delicate interbalance of the Earth's atmosphere is affected in India, causing the only cooking vessel in a poor family's hut to fall off its shelf and break.

We are interdependent. We were not born for ourselves alone. No one's life is an end in itself: it has a greater purpose, and is part of a greater whole. We need each other.

The story of the Ant and the Elephant tells of the ant who is on his way to an engagement, when he comes across the elephant, who is in his path.

'Excuse me', he squeaks.

The elephant doesn't hear. She continues to raise her trunk towards the sky and trumpet her pleasure at her size and strength. The ant goes away and returns with four other ants.

'Excuse me!' they chorus.

Still the elephant doesn't hear. The ants go away and return with forty-five other ants.

'Excuse me!!' they all shout together.

The elephant is so startled by the noise that she lumbers off, and the ant is then able to resume his journey.

There is an African proverb: when the foot gets a thorn in it, the whole body must stoop to get it out. We have a holy responsibility, given to us by God when we were created, for each other's wellbeing.

Thousands of years ago, the concept of the Jubilee Principle was written into the Bible (Leviticus 25:8f). It was a social ordering, given by God, to ensure there was a just and equitable distribution of wealth, and in order that the lending of money by the rich to the poor in their time of need did not enslave them. Every fifty years there was to be a cancelling of debts.

> 'Do not take advantage of each other, but fear your God. I am the Lord your God'.
> *Leviticus 25:17 (NIV)*

It is this principle of the Jubilee which, as I write, the Christian Churches and other concerned bodies are using to try to persuade governments and the World Bank to cancel the debts owed by the poorest Third World countries, as a creative way of marking the Millennium.

A broken chain has become a powerful symbol of the Jubilee 2000 campaign. When the G8 Summit was held in Birmingham in May 1998, many thousands of people linked hands in a human chain around the building in which the meeting was being held. Their action was symbolic of the chains which hold people in bondage as prisoners, and of the fact that when people join hands in order to work together, amazing things result.

On that fateful day, some hours before his neighbours dragged Jesus out and to the top of the hill with the intention of killing him:

> Jesus returned to Galilee powerful in the Spirit . . . He came to Nazareth where he had been reared. As he always did on the Sabbath, he went to the meeting place. When he stood up to read, he was handed the scroll of the prophet Isaiah. Unrolling the scroll, he found the place where it was written, 'God's Spirit is on me; he's chosen me to preach the Message of good news to the poor, sent me to announce pardon to prisoners and recovery of sight to the blind, to set the burdened and battered free, to announce, "This is God's year to act!"'
> *Luke 4:14f (The Message)*

For some time now, petitions have been signed in churches, and elsewhere, by those who feel strongly about this matter and who hope to persuade governments, and others in positions of relevant power, to cancel these debts. The interest payments on these loans alone often represent a huge percentage of a country's total income. Whilst they struggle to repay these moneys, vital basic work of education and raising low standards of health, hygiene and diet are having to be put on one side.

When my children were very small, I used to tell them the story of the old woman who went to market and bought a pig. The tale recounts all the myriad problems she had trying to get the pig home before night fell. However, nothing and nobody would co-operate with anyone or anything else, or with her. The old woman was nearly in despair.

Then, at last, just *one* thing changed. It was the mind of the cow. She decided, after all, to do as the old woman asked and, as a consequence, a whole chain of events was set in motion, resulting in the old woman getting home just as the sun disappeared below the horizon.

Although the structure of society and local communities has changed tremendously in the past fifty years, with many more people living a long way from relatives and the place in which they grew up – resulting in us all leading much more independent lives – we still seem to need each other as much as we ever did.

We're told, in this ever-more-computerised age, that most of the ordinary activities during which we make our casual encounters, such as shopping, will soon be done in the 'splendid isolation' of our living rooms. However, as the aftermath of the death of Diana, Princess of Wales showed, people's first instinct is still to come together for mutual support and sharing. During that week following Diana's death, the huge numbers which gathered together in their grief were responding to the deep human instinct *not* to be in isolation. It was obvious that so much comfort, hope and inspiration was shared in those acts of solidarity.

Each of us is in a variety of relationships. Some are constant, others change either frequently or occasionally. At the beginning of this book, there were drawings of two people, with a number of blank shapes floating about their heads. You were invited to imagine that the drawings were of yourself. The first drawing represents your external or outer relationships, and the invitation was to fill in the shapes with all your different current relationships and roles, for example, child/parent/neighbour, and so on. Even those who would describe themselves as loners will have filled in a number of shapes.

Each one of us is reflected in these relationships with others, and they in us. We are like mirrors held up to one another. We are born, live, grow and die in relationship.

Each one of us, in our turn, has a profound effect on others. Like widening ripples on a pool, when a pebble is dropped in, everyone's life has an influence on the whole world. Through our impact on others in our relationships, those people are affected and changed. They, in their turn, affect and change others. And so our influence on those whom we've never even met is perpetuated.

Some years ago, a group of psychologists established that stereotypes – the understanding and perception we have about various groups of people and things – were set far earlier than had originally been thought. The previous thinking had been that it took a number of contacts with a particular type of person or thing to build up an assumption, picture or stereotype. However, this research established that maybe just *one* contact was all that was needed in order to set up a firm stereotype in someone's mind.

If their findings are true, then that has very big implications indeed for the way in which we behave and relate to one another, for it is saying that each contact – however fleeting and maybe not even important enough to us to register consciously – goes to make up an overall picture. This will affect, in its turn, the way we perceive the world and so interact with it. And the same, of course, is true in reverse. Each one of us is shaped and formed by our relationships and our contact with others.

The communities with whom, and in which, we live form the context, the material, of who we are as individuals. They give us our meaning. This story of the Salt Doll is one of my favourites:

> A salt doll journeyed for thousands of miles over land, until it finally came to the sea. It was fascinated by this strange moving mass, quite unlike anything it had ever seen before.
>
> 'Who are you?' said the salt doll to the sea.
>
> The sea smilingly replied, 'Come in and see.'
>
> So the doll waded into the sea. The further it walked into the sea the more it dissolved, until there was only very little of it left. Before that last bit dissolved, the doll exclaimed in wonder,
>
> 'Now I know who I am!'
>
> (From *The Song of the Bird* by Anthony de Mello S.J. published by Guijarat Sahitya Prakash, Anand, India, 1983.)

The salt doll does not lose its individuality on entering the sea, but discovers that which truly complements it – and so discovers its true identity.

As we will see later, the mystery of the Trinity is this paradox of perfect union with perfect individuality. It is the paradox at the centre of all our relationships, and emulating it is our ongoing challenge.

Total absorption of our individuality into others is as bad as isolation. We need to retain a clear sense of who we are, for our individuality and uniqueness are a glorious gift from God. Equally we need to retain a clear sense of who we are in order that we do not lose our sense of personal responsibility for who and what we are, and for our actions.

To stay with the nautical analogy for just a moment more: I suspect many of us spend the majority of our lives like the fish who is swimming in the ocean but who keeps looking for the ocean.

It is difficult to imagine a world without relationships, each person insulated from everyone else and having no contact with, nor influence upon, the life of anyone else.

A friend once shared the following dream with me – well, it was more a nightmare, really. It was, she said, one of those dreams (or nightmares) which is so realistic that, for some time after you wake, you are unsure whether you are still in the dream; unsure of what is the reality. I tell it to you now as she told it to me:

> 'It was a post-nuclear-bomb world, barren and devastated.
> A great Arctic waste stretched in every direction as far as the eye could see, and a freezing wind blew continually.
> At first I thought I was alone in this desolate wasteland. Then I saw some other people and, with a glad cry, I reached out to them. Or, rather, I tried to. The reality was that the glad cry was only within myself. I could make no outer sound and, however hard I struggled, my arms, my whole body, seemed paralysed.
> As I gazed longingly at these people, who seemed to increase in number by the second, I realised that they too were struggling to reach out to me and to each other, but with no more success than I.
> As the timeless-time went by, I realised something else: the reason for our inability to move was a transparent film which covered each of us like a cocoon, immobilising each person and totally isolating her or him. Each of us could see, but would never be able to communicate with anyone else.
> We were all locked in a nightmare of non-communication and non-relationship.'
> (First told in *Woven Fine* by Susan Hardwick; Kevin Mayhew Ltd. 1997.)

It is a well-known fact that tiny babies who are not

touched and talked to regularly soon begin to pine away. Communication is essential to their survival; they are literally touched and talked into life in just the way, as we read in Genesis 1:1f, that God touched and talked creation into life.

I wonder – was it that first touch, those first words, which created in us such a longing, such a desire, for communication with one another? All the super-sophistication of our technological age has not replaced our basic need, which seems to have been implanted at the very centre of our genetic imprint, for the simple first-hand encounter, the meeting of eye or hand, the smile, the quiet word.

If we think of those relationships which are closest to us, they are usually the ones which give us the greatest joy, but also the deepest pain and hurt, because it is these people to whom we most fully open ourselves up and become most vulnerable. We cannot live in close proximity to others without pretences being stripped away, and our real selves being exposed.

It can be very painful, when we have poured in much effort and love, if others don't respond as we feel they ought, or as we had hoped. Why, though, *are* we surprised and so very disappointed? Maybe it is, in part, because we don't allow the other to be themselves, but want them to be the picture or fantasy we have created in our minds. Or, maybe, we want them to be like us; thinking like us, feeling like us, behaving and reacting like us. That way we can control them, and the situation or relationship.

However, true love really should be about loving people into freedom, into being their best selves and not into the image we have created for them.

Nowhere is this more clearly reflected than in parent/child relationships. Every parent of grown children will remember times of conflict when child/teenage will is set against parental will, as the younger person strives to assert their own independence and personality, and the older person their authority and will and wisdom. Much of the skill of good parenting seems to lie in discerning when to give in gracefully and when to stand firm.

As we have seen already, though, even Mary and Joseph seem to have struggled with this one, feeling puzzled and hurt by Jesus' assertion of his independence when he was twelve (Luke 2:41f). And, when he was a grown man Mary, now a widow, was often bewildered by his actions. Letting go of her son into his public ministry was obviously sometimes the cause of the sword, of which Simeon had warned her all those years ago, piercing her heart (Luke 2:35b).

Each of our relationships brings particular blessings and particular responsibilities. Our ongoing challenge, our lifelong task, is how best to live each one out. Yet, however difficult, turbulent or confusing we find our relationships, as a child of God each of us may draw upon his promise that, if we turn to him in trust and faith, he will do it:

> He who has called you is trustworthy and will carry it out.
> *I Thessalonians 5:24 (NJB)*

Part Three

Prayers

Carer

Remembering the personhood

It's an ever-present temptation
conveniently to forget,
degree by subtle degree,
that the person whose wants
I have to tend,
day after day after day,
needs my respect and my sensitivity
quite as much as the physical care
– if not even more.

So, help me, God,
in the seemingly endless round
of all that is to be done,
to acknowledge their personhood
– all that which makes them unique
and unlike any other.

To remember that,
in caring for them,
I meet with you
face to face.

A love proved

Constant God,
thank you.
Thank you for the chance
and the opportunity
to be able to demonstrate my feelings
in this way:
my love for her,
my love for you,
proved in this refiner's fire
of our present situation.

First and last thoughts

Jesus,
before you were
a teacher,
a healer,
a raiser of the dead,
you were a carer.

When you had finished
teaching,
and healing,
and raising,
you were still a carer.

'John,
behold your mother.
Woman,
behold your son':
your very last words were caring.

Help me to walk
in your way;
to follow the example
you have set.
To care as you have cared.

Friend

What it is to be human

Dear God,
from casual acquaintances
to my very closest friends:
a whole range of contacts
of different levels of intimacy.
With each one I share
more or less of myself
– and each one in return
gifts something of themselves to me.

Every time I see myself
mirrored in their response,
I understand a little more
of what it is to be human.
Thank you for the sweetness,
the manifold pleasures,
the lows and the highs,
the ups and the downs,
the privilege and blessings
of friendship.

A Judas kiss

I think I understand,
just a little now, Jesus,
of how you must have felt
when Judas betrayed you.
– One of your greatest and closest friends
willing to sell you
for thirty pieces of silver.

My 'friend's' betrayal of me
has rocked my world.
Help me not to lose faith and trust
in all the others.
Help me to be compassionate,
and one day to understand
and to forgive.

The friend above all other

Jesus –
when the world seems
barren of friends,
I remember you.

When the world seems
too busy to care,
I remember you.

You are
the friend above all other.
No one else
can take your place.

Neighbour

Who is *my neighbour?*

'Love your neighbour
as yourself':
the second part
of that great command.
But who *is* my neighbour?
Next door?
Next street?
Next town?

When you stretched wide your arms
upon your Cross, Jesus,
you embraced the world.
Is that then
your definition of neighbour?

Building the Kingdom

Greater God,
the hardest people to care for
can be those closest by,
for such proximity
can sometimes breed contempt
– or at least leave *no* illusions!

So give me tolerance
and a generous heart.
Open my eyes to see
how I may play my part
in building your Kingdom in this street.

A vision of the future

When Martin Luther King
stood shoulder to shoulder
with all of his people,
and declared his dream,
he didn't stop loving
those who oppressed him.
Teach me to have
such a brightness of vision.
To work for your world
as you meant it to be.
Where justice and equity rule
– and not status, or colour of skin.

Finding time for others

Jesus,
I read the tales
of your earthly life
and I wonder,
how *did* you manage it all?

So busy,
what with the world to heal
and to save,
yet still finding time
for those who came to you
as well as those in your care.

Was it because
you'd got your priorities right,
and so everything
somehow fell into place?

With your eyes fixed on God,
and feet firmly earth-planted,
you knew exactly
where first to go
and what first to do.

Offspring
Child/Teenager

My family

Jesus,
thank you for my family;
my parents, brothers, sisters,
aunts, uncles,
grandparents and cousins.
A whole band of people
surrounding, supporting
and loving me:
teaching me what it is
to be truly human
– providing a framework and context
within and against which
I can develop and grow
and discover who I am.

Just as I am

Everyone keeps telling me
'these are the best days'.
If this is true,
then I don't hold out
much hope for the future!
I'm a stranger to me,
and I feel like I'm a stranger
to everyone else.
It's a lonely and difficult time,
and never more have I needed you
than I do now, Jesus.
With you
I don't need to worry
whether I'm getting it right.
You accept me and love me
just as I am.
You are all in all to me.

Life's rich promise

With each new day that dawns,
I feel my world expand.
New opportunities,
new understandings,
new people,
plans for the future.

And all of it set
within your glorious Creation.

Your love for me
and for each one of us
is shown in a million different ways,
and teaches us in our turn
how it is we are to love
one another
and you.

Adult

Role reversal

Dad –
Once – it was your mother who patiently spooned food
into your mouth,
and you who spat out what you did not like.
Then – it was you who patiently spooned food
into my mouth,
and I who spat out what I did not like.
Now – it is I who patiently spoon food
into your mouth,
and you who dribble out what you do not like.

The circle has been completed.
The end has joined the beginning.
Dusk has met the dawn.
There is a poignant anguish
in this inverted parent-child relationship:
what you once did for me,
now I do for you;
tenderly, respectfully,
and with a sense of awe.
Personal tasks. Intimate tasks.

And I wonder –
Do you know?
Do you mind?
Do you care?
Behind that blank stare
do you know it is me?
(From *Woven Fine* by Susan Hardwick:
Kevin Mayhew Ltd. 1997)

Laying a deep foundation

Through all my childhood years,
sharing my tears and my celebrations,
dealing with teenage turbulence,
giving words of wisdom
– not always received with gratitude! –
they were so good and loving
in the task of raising me.
Now,
we share the pleasures and joys
of an adult relationship;
the foundation of those years
enriching and nourishing each encounter.
Heavenly Father,
I ask you to pour down your blessings
upon my earthly parents,
who have so tenderly, faithfully,
carried out their task.

Parent

Gift and joy

Dear God,
no one
– except another parent like you –
can fully understand
what it's like.
How it demands your all
– and then more.
How it stretches your patience,
your understanding,
and your love,
to the nth degree.
How it is the most amazing,
awesome and privileged calling
in the whole of creation
to be a parent.

Thank you.

Thank you
for the wondrous gift
and blessing,
and for the joy,
of my children.

Lament

I had such hopes and dreams
for him.
I wanted *so* much to 'be there'
for him.
I've tried so hard to get through
to him.
But, whatever I say, it's not right
for him.

Oh, God,
the taste of failure is bitter
to me.
Be as a beacon of hope
to me;
a guiding light of wisdom
for me.
Show me what I must do
if I am to break through
to him.
I beg
of you.

Lent, not given

Children are lent,
not given.
I always knew
the day would come
when I'd have to let go.
Now it's here,
and the tears
are mixed with the deepest pride.
It's been a task well done.
Yet within me I know

that my heart will never let go;
that my love and my child
are inextricably intertwined.
Being a parent is a life-sentence:
the day my child was born
my world changed forever.
But, truly, it has been
the sweetest of confinements.

Parent/Friend

My Heavenly Parent,
from the anxious nurture
of the new-born parent
for the new-born child,
through the delights and despairs
of caring through their growing years,
to the wonderful privilege
of their adult friendship.

Yet sometimes still
the pendulum subtly swings
between their need for equality
and their wish for gentle parenting.

As we each get older,
and perhaps the emphasis changes,
may our relationship
stay as fresh,
sweet and strong
as it is now,
at this present moment.

Partner

Is this the one?

After the years of searching,
of hopes raised
and then disappointed
can this really,
at last,
be *the* one for me?

Help me
to nurture this relationship:
not to burden it
with over-expectation,
and yet to give
of my very best.

Help me
to keep it fresh and new:
to respect and value our differences
and all that makes
my partner unique
– those qualities to which
I was drawn in the first place.

Help us
to love generously,
and with much delight.
Bless our union:
physical,
mental,
emotional
and spiritual.
In all that we think,
or say,
or do,
may we reflect
something of you.

The turning of the years

Through the turning of the years
our love has changed
for my partner and me.
The excitement and passion
of those early days
has given way
to a deep and steady rhythm.
Yet still my heart can quicken
and my blood run hot
for the one whose lot
I've shared for so long
– and who, with just a smile,
can turn night into day.
Thank you, God,
for the heavenly blessing
of my life-companion.
Such a gift
is a pearl beyond price.

Where did it all go wrong?

Where did it all go wrong?
There's now so much discord.
In every way we seem to be
dancing to a different tune.
Help us, Jesus.
Please help us to see.
Show us what we must do
to make things right;
the way they used to be.

Worker

God's human face

I pray for those
with whom I work.
In the busyness
of all that must be done
don't let me forget
that these relationships matter.

Thank you for the signs
of your presence in our midst:
the unexpected smile,
the quick word of congratulation,
the hand on the shoulder
in encouragement
or sympathetic solidarity,
the shared lightheartedness and humour
– moments which brighten the day
and give it humanity.

These are holy times,
which refocus and realign
our priorities and perspective.
They are reminders of you.
They are your human face.

From all walks of life

Jesus –
you called people
from all kinds of work
to go and follow you.
Outer status and position
did not impress,
but rather

the inner workings of the heart.
You treated each
and every one
with the same respect
and courtesy.
Help me to learn
this sacred lesson,
and to live it out
with those both more
and less senior to me.

My work is done for you

May I be a worker for you.

May I see my place of work
as a golden opportunity
to live out the values
of your Kingdom.

May you work through me
in my various relationships
with my colleagues.

Help me to 'render to Caesar'
that which is his:
an honest return of labour
for my pay.

Help me always to remember
that the whole world
– everyone, every place,
and everything within it -
is ordered under *your* direction,
and that *your* values should rule supreme.

May my work be done as for you.

Endings

Such a pain-filled time

Oh, God! –
This is such a pain-filled time.
My heart aches when I recall
the missed opportunities,
the ill-chosen words,
the actions - or inactions,
and so many other misjudged things
– on both sides –
that have led to this moment.

We are so in need
of your healing touch
upon this situation,
upon those caught up in it,
and upon the deep hurts
which have been inflicted.

May we find the grace
to part in peace.
As we go on our separate ways,
make our future paths straight.
As the bad memories heal and fade
may we only remember the good.
May all we have learned guide us
to do it better the next time.

The joy and privilege of our relationship

Jesus –
Thank you for the joy
and the privilege
of our relationship.
The ending was not of our choosing.
But the pain of parting
is shot through with smiles
of so many sweet
and marvellous memories.
Thank you
for the joy
and the privilege
of such a relationship.

An ending – and a beginning

As one door closes, another opens.
An ending implies also a beginning:
an open door of promise
and of opportunity.

God of hope –
walk through it with me.
Open my eyes to see
all the possibilities
which are there to be taken.
– Then open my mind
and my heart
to use them aright.

Beginnings

It's begun badly

We began this relationship badly.
Help us to change things
– ourselves and our attitudes included –
so that negative
may be turned into positive,
and your way of love
direct us from now on.

The start of something good?

Bless this beginning,
Lord.
May it be the start
of something good.
May generosity,
and sensitivity,
towards the needs
of each other
be our guiding rule.

When the first glow goes

There's a whole world of promise
in starting something new.
Nothing has yet happened
to take the glow away.
When that time comes,
– as surely it must,

for that is the way of relationships –
please give us the wisdom
to handle it,
and to build creatively upon it,
so that something even deeper,
and richer,
may be the result.

Separation

A trial separation

'A trial separation':
that's precisely what it is
– a trial.
The dictionary defines that as
'the process of testing
the qualities of a thing'.
Our time apart has taught me
the true value of what
I once took so much for granted.

Help me not to make
the same terrible mistake again.
Help me from now on
truly to value that
which is precious in my life.
Forgiving Lord,
forgive me for not seeing it,
and for not doing it,
before.

May the time pass quickly

Protector God –
The situation has dictated
we must be apart.
Bless and guard her.
Keep her safe and well.
May the time pass quickly
until we can be together once more.

Distance doesn't really *matter*

Lord of space –
this separation has proved
distance doesn't really matter:
that we are linked on other planes
than just the purely physical.
Thank you for the heavenly gift
and the blessing
of a relationship such as ours;
when being apart merely reinforces
and deepens feelings and commitment.

Hurts

Cocooned in our own separate pain

Jesus –
I've hurt him.
He's hurt me.
Now we're both cocooned
in our own separate pain.
Physically side by side
but emotionally oh, *so* distant.

Give us the grace
to breech the barriers.
Let understanding and forgiveness
flow freely in.

The hurt I've inflicted

Forgiving God,
forgive me the hurt I've inflicted.
Give me the wisdom to know
how I may make it right.

A growth point

Why is that, so often,
the most painful moments
turn out to be growth points?
Jesus, Healer –
may it be so now.
May the pain we've felt
give birth to positive gain.

Joys

Those who colour each day

Most generous God,
thank you
for the special people in my life.
Those precious ones
who colour each day
with myriad shades and hues.
Who gift and bless me

with so much loving and caring.
And who draw out from me
abundant caring and loving in return.
May I never,
for even a moment,
take them at all for granted.

Perfect love casts out fear

There's an insidious fear
in the midst of my joy
in this relationship.
It is the fear of losing it;
of it all going wrong in some way.
That such a wondrous thing
is surely not destined to last,
and the fear of the pain
if that should happen

God of love,
there's a vulnerability
in such a loving as ours.
Help me so to direct
all of my energies
into nurturing this precious gift
that there is no room for fear.

Eyes to see and a heart that's open

Jesus,
May I have the eyes to see
the potential for joy
in each relationship.
May I have the courage

to reach out and to find it.
May I have a heart that's open
and ready to receive it.
May I know the joy
of your presence,
and see your face
in each person I meet.

God and us

Before the world began

My heavenly Father –
before the world began
you called my name.
You have loved me
into existence,
and your love now
sustains me in being.
We are tightly woven,
you and I.
With you,
I am everything.
Without you,
I am nothing.

I feel distant from you

Others speak of your nearness
– but my experience is
too often the opposite:
'Closer to me
than I am to myself'
is how others describe

their relationship with you.
Then why isn't it like that for me?
Why do you seem so distant?
Is it your fault?
Or is it mine?
Open my mind.
Open my heart.
Open my life.
Make me a fit dwelling place for you.
Come to me,
Lord Jesus.
Please come to me.

Always seeking you

Faithful God,
teach me constancy
and teach me faithfulness,
that I may never stop
seeking you.

Trusting enough to share everything

All-seeing God –
You,
who see the secrets
of all our hearts,
teach me so to trust you
that I will always tell you
the way it really is;
the way it really feels;
the joy, the pain,
the sadness,
the bewilderment, the longing,
and the anger, too.

Gather up these fragments.
Mould them. Shape them.
Bless and recreate them
in the furnace of your love.

I love you – but . . .

I love you –
but my love
could be
so much more.
Teach me
to love you,
as you
have first
loved me.

You are in control

'I shall instruct you
and teach you the way to go;
I shall not take my eyes off you.'*
Your hold is firm upon my life.
Take my hand.
Lead me where you will.
You are my friend;
closer to me than I am to myself.
You are my Lord.
You are my God.
**Psalm 32:8 (NJB)*

PART FOUR

THREE-WAY LOVE

One-In-Three

I AM . . . God

I AM is God's name for himself.
. . . The dots represent everything we can ever think to say about God – and more. Much, much more: for God is really beyond description.

Even our wonderful and beautiful and vast English language, with a word to express each of many shades of a particular meaning, fades into a silence as suitable words are searched and striven for, but not found. This is why wordless reflection and adoration, or contemplation as it is often called, seem for many such an appropriate and right way to sing God's praises for all that he is and has made: this amazing and wondrous world, and all the amazing and wondrous things within it.

I shall never forget, as a small child, the absolute delight and sheer wonder I felt when I first looked into a kaleidoscope, and the sense of power as, with just a twist of my hand, I transformed static blocks of colour into dancing, spinning rainbows of breathtaking beauty.

And I, a small child, had helped to create that miracle!

Further miracles awaited discovery. Each time I set the kaleidoscope spinning, new patterns were discovered. Each colour was subdivided into many, many more shades. It was never the same twice. Like snowflakes, each time it was unique: never-to-be-repeated.

Looking back from my vantage point as an adult, I can see that the kaleidoscope experience was part of my childhood understanding of God and his creation. If I, a small child, could create such beauty out of ordinary raw materials with just a twist of my hand, how much more so could God. And, like the kaleidoscope, no pattern would be repeated.

But *he* needed *me* too. ME: a tiny child, yet still important, essential even, to God's purpose for the world. He needed me to turn the kaleidoscope, to activate the process. I had to become a partner in his creation.

All my life, since then, I have been constantly caught up by, and in, the absolute wonder of God's creation. Sometimes, when I walk in the countryside, or beside the sea, I feel so drawn into and absorbed by its beauty, that I am one with it. My identity feels as though it fuses with it, and I forget who I am – and very often, indeed, *where* I am!

Each human being, each living creature, all of God's creation from mighty mountains to the last blade of grass, was created by his love, in love. As human beings, we are created:

- To love him;
- To love ourselves;
- To love each other.

> Our Lord Jesus Christ said:
>
> 'The first commandment is this: . . . The Lord your God is the only Lord. You shall love the Lord your God with all your heart, with all your soul, with all your mind, and with all your strength.
>
> The second is this: Love your neighbour as yourself. There is no other commandment greater than these.' (*Summary of the Law:* ASB. A. R. Mowbray and Co Ltd. 1980.)

> Jesus said – 'I give you a new commandment: love one another; you must love one another just as I have loved you. It is by your love for one another that everyone will recognise you as my disciples'.
> *John 13:34f (NJB)*

Three-In-One

WE ARE . . . the Father, the Son and the Holy Spirit

We get our understanding of community, in fact, from God. He is, himself, in community with his Son, Jesus Christ, and The Holy Spirit. Three separate beings, but all intimately interlinked and absolutely equal – so at one with each other that none could co-exist without the others.

The mystery of the Trinity, as we have already reflected, is this paradox of perfect union with perfect individuality. How can it possibly be so? Three in one? And one in three? It seems so mindbending, and very difficult indeed *really* to imagine.

Three in one, and one in three sounds like a motto for the Three Musketeers, or a cryptic clue in a particularly difficult crossword. It is many preachers' annual nightmare to try to write a sensible and useful sermon year after year on the Trinity, and one which manages to say something new and enlightening.

For, once again, as so often when we try to define and describe God, we stumble for adequate and appropriate words, as we attempt to embody in human terms truths that which really can only be wondered at in the silent worship of the heart.

But, if we unpick the fabric of the idea, so to speak, and look at the different threads, an amazing picture does begin to emerge.

Firstly, how can *three* people be *one*? Even in our limited human experience, many of us know intimate moments when we are so close to another human being that it feels as if two separate beings have fused into one. Lovers, or a mother cuddling her child, are just two examples.

There is a sense of rightness, of completeness and fulfilment at these times which seems to indicate that, in that union, we see something of our destiny as humans. And, in that wonder and delight and harmony, we feel we have touched the edge of the real meaning of the word 'joy'.

'One in three' seems a bit easier to grasp emphasising, as it does, the individuality and separateness of the three within the close relationship.

During my early teens, I had two particularly close friends and, as we were usually seen together, we were eventually dubbed 'the trinity'.

The more time we spent together, the closer we became. And the closer we became, the more we understood and valued each other. And yet, each was so very different from the other two, and remained so. We were quite distinct.

None of us had any desire whatsoever to become the same as the others. However, over a period of time, I think in many ways we really did become one in three. No one person dominated the trio; each of us felt fully equal and equally important to the success of the friendship.

Some of the elements that drew us ever closer and cemented our friendship were those things that are part of any successful relationship:

- Natural affinity.
- Proximity.
- Need and desire for companionship.
- Mutual caring.
- Generosity.
- Kindness.
- Thoughtfulness.
- Awareness: of each other's needs, and of the privilege of such a friendship, and the consequent responsibility to value the gift.
- Humour.
- Tolerance.
- A growing and deepening love for one another.
- Respect: for each other's differences, and points of view, and way of doing and saying things, which may be very

different from one's own way – but seeing that as a growing point, and an opportunity to widen understanding.

- Being real . . .

Of course much, if not all, the above could be applied to any deep relationship.

It is by experiencing relationships with other human beings that we are brought closer to understanding the relationship of God the Father with his Son Jesus Christ, and the Holy Spirit – who, in their turn, point us back again to the importance of close and loving human relationships.

One difficulty with the Trinity is that, over the centuries, certain theologians have claimed a monopoly of understanding and interpretation. Too often, they have drained all life out by dry-as-dust pronouncements in inaccessible language, which is so specialised that only the initiated have any hope of comprehending. And so understanding of the Trinity has been removed from many people.

Perhaps we need a campaign to 'Reclaim the Trinity'.

Four-Way Love

WE ARE . . . The Trinity – and us

Like many people, my experience of the Father is as a tender, loving, forgiving God who, nonetheless, expects the very best I can be and give.

My experience of Jesus is as the Saviour who spent his earthly life teaching me how to live, and who loved me enough then to die for me, before rising from the dead and raising me to new life with him.

My experience of the Holy Spirit is that which lives in me, closer to me than I am to myself, and who is my inspiration, my comforter and support, my God-energy and my God-guide.

If these three experiences reflect at all the reality, then the combination and compacting of all of this life-force into one must result in such a dense concentration of love and joy which could burst through our human-erected barriers and flood God's creation, if only we would let it.

If the three really are one then, if the Holy Spirit dwells in me, so must the other two. If the God-Trinity dwells in me, closer to me than I am to myself, then I must have the potential to do God-like things:

> '. . . those who hope in the Lord will renew their strength. They will soar on wings like eagles . . .'
> *Isaiah 40:31a (NIV)*

When we try to express how and what we feel about God, we use words and statues and carved items and paintings, and so on. However, there comes a time when paintings, words, and suchlike, can say no more. It is at this point that we have to move from head to heart. We have to enter into silence, and allow God's word to speak in our heart.

If we wait faithfully upon God, seeking in all things to do his will, there will come a time when we . . .

> . . . suddenly recognise that God is a living, personal presence, not a piece of chiselled stone. And when God is personally present, a living Spirit, that old, constricting legislation is recognised as obsolete. We're free of it! All of us! Nothing between us and God, our faces shining with the brightness of his face. And so we are transfigured much like the Messiah,* our lives gradually becoming brighter and more beautiful as God enters our lives and we become like him.
> *2 Corinthians 3:16f (The Message)*
> **Matthew 17:1f; Mark 9:2f; Luke 9:28f*

Another translation puts it like this:

> . . . Now this Lord is the Spirit, and where the Spirit of the Lord is, there is freedom. And all of us, with our unveiled faces like mirrors reflecting the glory of the Lord, are being transformed into the image that we reflect in brighter and brighter glory; this is the working of the Lord who is Spirit.
> *2 Corinthians 3:17f (NJB)*

God's relationship with all he has made

God is at the very centre, the very heart of his creation, and of each one of us.

He is also beyond all he has made.

As our minds and brains push out the boundaries of our understanding, God is ever before us; wider, deeper, more vast and immense than anything we will ever discover in this life. The eternal God is beyond the limitations of space and time; beyond the limitations of our human measuring.

The God who can be tenderly and intimately present to me, and in me, is also the God of the storm and the tempest . . .

> . . . He parted the heavens and came down, a storm-cloud underneath his feet; . . . soaring on the wings of the wind . . . *Psalm 18:9, 10 (NJB)*

He is the God also of the cosmos, who speaks to Job from the heart of the tempest, reminding him of his supremacy as Creator of all that is . . .

'. . . Where were you when I laid the earth's foundations?
Who decided its dimensions, or who stretched the measuring line across it?
What supports its pillars at their bases?·
Who laid its cornerstone to the joyful concert of the morning stars?

'Who pent up the sea behind closed doors
when it leapt tumultuous from the womb,
when I wrapped it in a robe of mist,
and made black clouds its swaddling bands?

'Have you ever in your life given orders to the morning
or sent the dawn to its post?
Which is the way to the home of the Light,
and where does darkness live?

'Who begets the dewdrops?
What womb brings forth the ice,
who gives birth to the frost of heaven?

'Can your voice carry as far as the clouds
and make the pent-up waters do your bidding? . . .'
Job 38:4f (NJB: extracts)

More than 3,000 years ago God, as a pillar of fire, led the Israelites safely through the desert. At last, they stood at the edge of the Promised Land.

Moses said to them:

'. . . the Lord your God is a consuming fire . . .'
Deuteronomy 4:24 (NJB)

Some 1,300 years later, in the first century AD, a letter was written to the Hebrews. The author stresses that the pilgrimage of the Israelites through the desert was an image of the Christian pilgrimage to the final place of rest; and that the faith of the great patriarchs, such as Moses, was a model for Christian faith and perseverance . . .

> . . . Come to Mount Zion, to the heavenly Jerusalem, the city of the living God . . . come to God, the judge of all people . . . to Jesus, the mediator of a new covenant . . . Let us be thankful, and so worship God acceptably with reverence and awe, for our 'God is a consuming fire'.
> *Hebrews 12:22f (NJB)*

The Last Word

No matter what I say, what I believe,
    and what I do, I'm bankrupt without love.
Love never gives up.
Love cares more for others than for self.
Love doesn't want what it doesn't have.
Love doesn't strut,
Doesn't have a swelled head,
Doesn't force itself on others,
Isn't always 'me first',
Doesn't fly off the handle,
Doesn't keep score of the sins of others,
Doesn't revel when others grovel,
Takes pleasure in the flowering of the truth,
Puts up with anything,
Trusts God always,
Always looks for the best,
Never looks back,
Keeps going to the end.
Love never dies.
I Corinthians 13:3f (The Message)

I first came across the following exercise many years ago. It never ceases to challenge me each time I do it.

- Read through the above as it is written.
- Then read through, a second time, substituting the name of Jesus for the word 'love'.
- Finally, read through substituting your own name for 'love'.

Dear God –

You are the One
who loved us into existence.

You are the One
from whose womb we came.

You are the One
who calls us now,
and through eternity,
into a relationship
so close that,
one day,
we will become absorbed
into you . . .

. . . For your love
is a consuming fire.
Amen.

Jesus said, 'A new commandment I give to you:
That you love one another as I have loved you. . .
My command to you is to love one another'.
John 13:34f (NIV)